Freedom
of Belief

Mike Hirst

SEA-TO-SEA
Mankato Collingwood London

This edition first published in 2006 by
Sea-to-Sea Publications
1980 Lookout Drive
North Mankato
Minnesota 56003

Printed in China

Library of Congress Cataloging-in-Pubication Data

Hirst, Mike.
  Freedom of belief/by Mike Hirst
    p. cm. — (What do we mean by human rights?)
  Includes index.
  ISBN 1-932889-66-3
    1. Freedom of religion—Juvenile literature. 2. Human rights—Juvenile
  literature. I. Title. II. Series.

BL640.H57 2005
323.44'2—dc22

                                                        2004063641

9 8 7 6 5 4 3 2

Published by arrangement with the Watts Publishing Group Ltd, London

Acknowledgments:

Palden Gyatso, *The Guardian*, March 9, 1995; http:www.themoscowtimes.com/stories/2004/06/03/004.html and http://news.bbc.co.uk/2/hi/europe/3768975.stm; Ken Saro-Wiwa, *The Observer*, November 3, 1995, *The Guardian*, November 11, 1995, *The Sunday Times*, November 12, 1995; Bob Dent, *The Daily Telegraph*, October 26, 1996; Pensacola clinic, *The Independent*, September 10, 1994, *The Sunday Times*, June 18, 1995; Ayodhya temple, *The Guardian*, December 7 & 8, 1992, *The Independent on Sunday*, December 13, 1992; Zlata Filipovic *Zlata's Diary*, Viking Penguin, 1994; http://www.cfpni.org/newsletters/papers/2004_Spring.pdf; http://www.nytimes.com/2004/06/10/nyregion/10matters.html?pagewanted=print&position=]; Margarethe Cammermeyer, Edmund Hall, *We Can't Even March Straight*, Verso, 1995.

Picture credits:

Cover and title page: Panos Pictures (Jean-Leo Dugast)
Amnesty International, UK, 43T; Camera Press 8BR (Makaslini), 33B (Sir Russell Johnson); *The Guardian* 6 (Sean Smith); Hulton Getty 10T, 10B, 15T & B; The Hutchinson Library 31B, 39 (Crispin Hughes); KATZ 26B (Steve Mayer/*Pensacola News Journal*/SABA), 26T (Gary McCracken/*Pensacola News Journal*/SABA), 35 (David Modell); The Image Bank 29T (Gerard Champlong); Magnum Photos 16B (James Nachtwey), 29B (Abbas), 34B (N. Economopoulos); Mary Evans Picture Library 9L, 14T & B, 20, 21L, 27B; Panos Pictures 12 (Neil Cooper), 18B (Betty Press), 19 (Alberto Arzoz); Popperfoto/AFP 11T; Rex Features Ltd. 7R (Herbie Knott), 13T (Kazuyoshi Nomachi), 17 (Tom Stockhill), 22T (R Trippett/Sipa Press), 23T & B (Skyscans), 24T & B (David Hancock), 27T (Blanche), 28 (Sipa Press), 31T (Sipa Press), 32 (Alexandra Boulay/Sipa Press), 33T (Shone/Sipa Press), 34T (Alexandra Boulay/Sipa Press), 36T, 37T (Sipa Press), 37B (Alan Lewis), 38 (Shane Owen), 40T (Cygne/Sipa Press), 40B (Kessler/Sipa Press), 41 (David Sams/Sipa Press), 42 (Sipa Press), 43 (Sipa Press); Robert Harding 18T, 36B (E Simanor); Topham 7L (Associated Press), 8T, 8BL (Press Association/Sean Dempsey) 13B, 16T, 21T, 22B; TRIP 11B (D. Oliver); ZEFA 9R (M.M. Lawrence), 25T, 25B (A. Leonard). Map of former Yugoslavia provided by Julian Baker Illustrations.

CONTENTS

Valuing freedom of belief   6

Life without freedom   13

Governments and people   20

Communities in conflict   28

Living together   38

Glossary   44

Useful addresses   45

Index   46

VALUING FREEDOM OF BELIEF

Place:
Tibet/China
Date:
1950-Today
Issue:
Living by your
beliefs

In 1950, Communist Chinese forces took over Tibet, a large but thinly populated country high in the Himalayan mountains. Tibet is a Buddhist country and for most of its history its leaders have been Buddhist priests from one of Tibet's main monasteries.

Many Tibetans have opposed Chinese control of their country. Some object to the Communist political system which allows only one political party. Others feel that their traditional culture and way of life is being destroyed by China.

"Ceaselessly, I will speak about these things until I die."

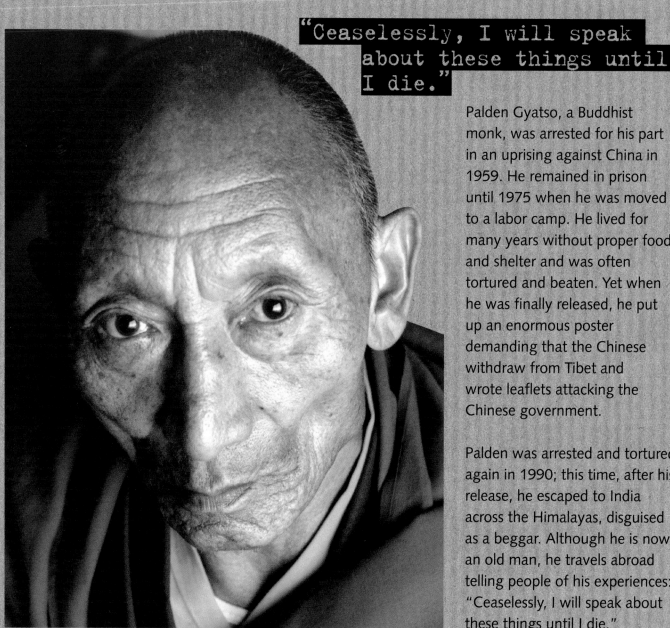

Palden Gyatso, a Buddhist monk, was arrested for his part in an uprising against China in 1959. He remained in prison until 1975 when he was moved to a labor camp. He lived for many years without proper food and shelter and was often tortured and beaten. Yet when he was finally released, he put up an enormous poster demanding that the Chinese withdraw from Tibet and wrote leaflets attacking the Chinese government.

Palden was arrested and tortured again in 1990; this time, after his release, he escaped to India across the Himalayas, disguised as a beggar. Although he is now an old man, he travels abroad telling people of his experiences: "Ceaselessly, I will speak about these things until I die."

What are beliefs?

Palden Gyatso has spent much of his life in prison because his political beliefs were different from those of the people who govern his country—and because he feels that, under Chinese rule, he cannot fully and openly practice his Buddhist religion.

Like these refugee children, many Tibetan Buddhists now live in India.

(Right) For Muslims, freedom of belief includes being able to pray 5 times a day.

What we "believe" covers an enormous number of different thoughts and ideas. Many people have strong beliefs about politics, for example. Like Palden Gyatso, they believe that some kinds of government are right, while others are wrong. They may face great hardship because they refuse to accept a system of government with which they cannot agree.

"teachings and traditions"

Religious ideas are another form of belief that are central to many people's lives, and much of the world's population follows a religion such as Islam, Christianity, or Hinduism. If you do observe a religion, you will try to lead your life according to its teachings and traditions. Your religion may affect the clothes you wear, the food you eat, and possibly even the language in which you say your prayers. Your faith will also provide you with a set of beliefs about what is right and wrong, and teach you what is a good way to behave.

Strong views

However, just because someone is not "religious" does not mean that he or she may not also have deeply held views. That person may, for instance, have strong ideas about how we should behave toward other people or how we should treat animals or the environment.

In fact, everyone thinks that some kinds of behavior are acceptable while others are not. Most people, for example, believe that it is wrong to steal. Philosophers have a name for these ideas about right and wrong: ethics.

Each person has their own system of ethics, which may come from a variety of different sources. Our beliefs about right and wrong may be based on a religion, what our parents have taught us, or what we have worked out for ourselves—or a combination of all three. Wherever they come from, our ethical ideas will have a major influence on the rest of our lives.

Is belief important?

Our beliefs about right and wrong affect the whole way that we choose to behave: what we believe influences what we do.

If you think, for instance, that it is cruel to kill animals to provide humans with meat you are likely to become a vegetarian. If, on the other hand, you think that killing animals for their meat is acceptable, you will probably eat meat. Our actions and attitudes are determined by our thoughts, beliefs, and ideas. In some countries people take the freedom to choose what they believe for granted; but many other people, like Palden Gyatso, have to fight for their freedom of belief.

Protesting against the killing of animals for their fur, this animal rights activist demonstrates against the start of the Canadian seal hunt.

Mahatma Gandhi used the peaceful technique of mass civil disobedience in his campaign for Indian independence. Such nonviolent methods are powerful ways to put across the strength of your beliefs.

Some people eat vegetarian food because they believe it is wrong to kill animals for meat.

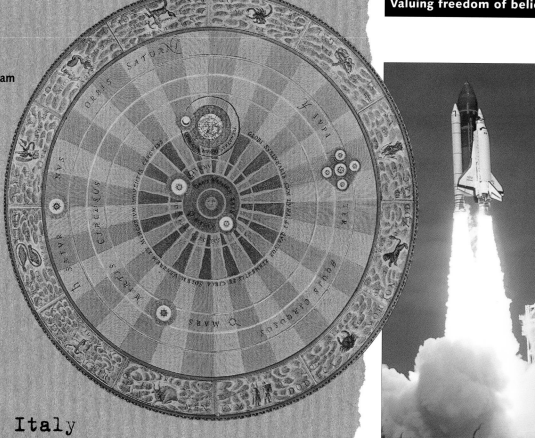

This early diagram of the universe according to Copernicus shows clearly that the Earth goes around the Sun.

Copernicus's discoveries were important steps in our understanding of science and its laws, which would eventually lead to the exploration of space.

Place: Italy
Time: 1500–1600
Issue: The importance of freedom of thought

One of the most important scientific discoveries of all time was made by a Polish astronomer named Nicolas Copernicus (1473–1543). He was the first person to realize that the Earth is just one of the planets in the solar system, moving in an orbit around the Sun.

During the 1500s, however, powerful leaders of the Roman Catholic Church still believed that the Earth was at the center of the universe. Copernicus knew that his beliefs would upset the Church so he did not write about his discovery until just before he died.

Several years later, another scientist, Giordano Bruno, began to teach Copernicus's discovery. He was made an outcast by the Church, but refused to stop teaching what he believed was the truth. Eventually, he was arrested in Italy. He refused to say that Copernicus had been wrong, so in 1600 the Roman Catholic Church had him burned to death at the stake.

"burned to death"

The basis of progress

Freedom of thought is an important part of progress, scientific, political, social, or otherwise. People must be able to question old ideas and beliefs if they are ever to make new discoveries about the world in which we live. Giordano Bruno's bravery in teaching Copernicus's new understanding about the universe meant that the people who came after him could go on to make further important scientific discoveries.

9

Protecting our beliefs

Over the centuries, many people have come to recognize that freedom of belief is so important it should be considered a right for every individual worldwide. They are convinced that it is a right that needs protecting.

In Nazi Germany, and in the countries occupied by the Nazis in the Second World War, different groups in European society were relentlessly persecuted under the Nazi government. People's dignities were stripped away; those who

(Above) This man protested about the treatment of the Jewish community under the Nazi regime. He was beaten and forced to walk through the streets of Munich wearing a placard that read, "I am a Jew but I will never again complain about the Nazis."

At the Nuremberg trials after the Second World War, Nazi leaders were brought to justice for the atrocities they had committed.

10

held beliefs that opposed the Nazis were arrested and often killed. The systematic imprisonment and killing of Jewish people and people from other ethnic or minority groups appalled the world. Politicians in many countries wanted to find a way of stopping such events ever happening again. The United Nations was formed after the war to help countries work together to resolve their differences peacefully. In 1948, the member states of the United Nations adopted the Universal Declaration of Human Rights.

Putting freedom into practice

Almost all of the world's states are members of the United Nations. Almost all countries in the world have signed the Universal Declaration of Human Rights. The basic rights listed in the Declaration are intended for all individuals to enjoy throughout the world, including the right to freedom of belief (see page 12). However, the move toward freedom of belief for everyone has not been quick or easy. Tolerating freedom of thought has been much easier for some countries to achieve than others.

In many parts of the world, governments are frightened of what may happen if their citizens are allowed complete freedom of belief; citizens might, after all, use this freedom to attack the government.

The United Nations General Assembly meets in New York. When important issues, such as human rights and world peace, are discussed all the member states usually attend the meetings.

"complete freedom of belief"

Boris Yeltsin, who became Russia's president in 1992, wanted to give Russian people more freedom than they had ever had.

Fundamental freedoms

Even when a country's leaders are genuinely committed to the idea of freedom of belief, granting this liberty to everyone may still cause some awkward problems. What should a government do, for instance, when one person's (or group's) beliefs bring them into conflict with other people? And are there, in fact, times when governments are justified in putting limits on how citizens "manifest" their beliefs?

The Dalai Lama is the exiled religious leader of Tibet's Buddhists. He has often spoken out in support of freedom of belief for everyone.

This is the main clause of the Universal Declaration of Human Rights that is concerned with freedom of belief:

Article 18
Everyone has the right to freedom of thought, conscience, and religion; this right includes freedom to change his religion or belief, and freedom, either alone or in community with others and in public or private, to manifest his religion or belief in teaching, practice, worship, and observance.

Article 18 of the Universal Declaration of Human Rights really tries to protect two fundamental freedoms: first, to allow each individual to choose a system of beliefs and ethics for him or herself; and, second, to allow everyone to live their lives as far as possible according to their beliefs.

This book looks at some of the problems surrounding freedom of belief, and finds out how and why people have tried to put Article 18 into practice.

LIFE WITHOUT FREEDOM

Time: 2004
Place: Russia
Issue: Freedom of expression

During the 20th century, millions of Soviet citizens were imprisoned in labor camps because their political ideas were different from those of the Soviet government.

Leonid Parfyonov was one of Russia's most popular and critical television journalists until June 2004. That was when he was fired and his popular news review program axed in the latest move by President Vladimir Putin to restore the authority of the state. After the fall of communism, the Russian media were reborn as free voices. There is still no official censorship, but the government has clamped down on independent journalists, who are learning to censor themselves.

Parfyonov's channel, NTV, was Russia's first independent television station, but was taken over in 2001 by a state-run company. When Parfyonov broadcast an interview with the widow of a killed Chechen

> "he was fired because he did not support the policies of the leadership"

rebel leader, he was fired because he did not "support the policies of the company's leadership." Yelena Savina, a producer for NTV's evening news program, said, "We, as newspeople, understand that this serious attack is a warning for us." And Parfyonov, who said he expected it sooner or later, added: "I do not need too be taught to love my Motherland."

This poster from the Russian Revolution symbolizes the power of the common people against the government.

Pictured here in Moscow's Red Square, Vladimir Ilyich Lenin became the Communist leader of the Russian Revolution in 1917.

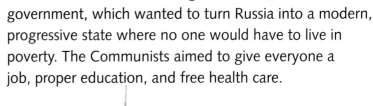

A totalitarian regime

A "totalitarian" regime is a regime where one leader or political party tries to control every aspect of citizens' lives. Adolf Hitler's Nazi government in Germany from 1933 to 1945 was one such totalitarian regime. Under such a government human rights, especially the right to freedom of belief, are often overlooked or even actively ignored.

There are still many countries in the world today that are more or less totalitarian; often poverty and historical influences have made it difficult to develop a society with freedom of belief. One of these historical influences has been Communism.

Revolutionary progress vs. Free thought?

In 1917 Russia was a country ruled by a small number of wealthy people; most of the population lived as poor peasants or factory workers. The Revolution of 1917 brought in a new, Communist government, which wanted to turn Russia into a modern, progressive state where no one would have to live in poverty. The Communists aimed to give everyone a job, proper education, and free health care.

Yet it quickly became clear that the Communist Party would not allow freedom of thought in the new Soviet Union. Soviet leaders believed that free thought would get in the way of building a better society. A totalitarian regime was developed under the Communist leader Joseph Stalin with punishments of death or imprisonment or for anyone who opposed the Party. The Communist Party insisted that freedom of thought was not possible if the country was to progress to higher standards of living.

An improved lifestyle

Many Russians agree that Communism may have improved living conditions for people in the Soviet Union, but,

"forced to choose"

it was also impossible without the freedom to think and believe what they wanted: "We were forced to choose from the very beginning…either to save our personalities, our souls, and give up our bodies, or do the opposite: save our bodies and give our personalities to be destroyed. In a totalitarian society you can't save both…"

(Above) Joseph Stalin became leader of the Communist Party of the Soviet Union in 1922.

(Right) Russian author Alexander Solzhenitsyn was expelled from Russia in 1974 for speaking out against the state.

A change in policy

Real changes in the Soviet Union did not come until after 1985, when Mikhail Gorbachev became leader and began an enormous program of change. He revised many of the country's systems, and, at the same time, insisted that freedom of thought should be permitted. In fact, he actually said that without freedom or "openness"—in Russian, *glasnost*—no other reform was possible.

Mikhail Gorbachev explains his new political policies to Soviet women in 1989.

The policy of *glasnost* in the Soviet Union allowed more political freedom in other parts of Eastern Europe. In Berlin, the wall (below) which had divided the Communist-controlled east of the city from the western sector was pulled down in 1989.

The process of change is still going on both in the countries of the former Soviet Union and Eastern Europe—which was dominated by the Soviet Union from 1945. All of the former Communist nations are today democracies and some are now part of the European Union, but many Eastern European countries have enormous economic difficulties to overcome.

However, there has been a radical move toward greater freedom of thought for individual people, and politicians no longer believe that they must choose between freedom of belief or economic progress. They are trying to build governments that attempt to give their citizens two major freedoms at once: the economic freedom of decent standards of living, and freedom of belief.

Place:
Nigeria
Time:
1995
Issue:
The right to act on
your beliefs

Ken Saro-Wiwa was an award-winning Nigerian novelist and TV dramatist, who for many years spoke out against his country's governments. He became particularly involved in fighting for better treatment for his own community, the Ogoni people who live in the oilfields in Rivers State in the Niger Delta.

Although their traditional home provides most of Nigeria's oil money, the Ogonis are among the poorest people in the country. Much of their land has been polluted by waste from oil wells and refineries and some of their villages have been demolished. Ken Saro-Wiwa spoke out for his people—acting on his belief that they were being wrongly treated.

"Freedom for citizens"

Ken Saro-Wiwa was a man of peace and "prisoner of conscience." The Nigerian government accused him of encouraging a political riot by young Ogonis in which four Nigerian chiefs were killed, although Saro-Wiwa was more than 90 miles away from the incident when it took place. He was unfairly tried and then hanged by the Nigerian authorities.

After General Sani Abacha seized power in Nigeria in November 1993, there was a clamp down on political opposition. Ken Saro-Wiwa was imprisoned several times. In 1995 he was arrested again and was charged with crimes that were never tried fairly in an open court. On November 10, 1995, Ken Saro-Wiwa was executed by hanging in Port Harcourt jail.

Many countries still put severe limits on the amount of freedom of belief they allow their citizens. In Africa, Asia, and South America, many governments are frightened to allow freedom of thought in case citizens criticize their rulers.

"Good" and "bad" nations

It is all too easy for people in more wealthy, democratic countries (where the government is elected for the people by the people) to tell the governments in poorer, developing nations that they should grant their citizens all the freedoms contained in the Universal Declaration of Human Rights.

In fact, we cannot divide today's world into "good" nations, which support human rights, and "bad" ones, which do not. Citizens' human rights are regularly violated by the governments of many of the member states of the United Nations, whether rich or poor, and with widely differing political and religious beliefs.

"oppressive governments"

The modern world is linked by a complicated network of trade and industry. Businessmen and politicians from wealthy, "free" countries may sometimes indirectly support oppressive governments in other parts of the globe. This was the situation that Ken Saro-Wiwa was trying to bring to the world's attention.

This ornate mosque (left) is an example of the generous investment by the Nigerian government in the country's new capital, Abuja. This level of investment does not seem to stretch to the local communities, (above), however.

Corruption and wealth

Since the 1960s, Nigeria has been ruled by a succession of military dictators. Many have been, to some extent, corrupt. Much of the wealth generated by the country's oil industry has been used by the ruling parties to buy weapons in order to stay in power.

"our human rights are interlinked"

The oil reserves have been exploited by several multinational oil companies, with the local population receiving few benefits. After Ken Saro-Wiwa's execution, demonstrators in Europe tried to put pressure on the oil industry to stop trading in Nigeria unless the Nigerian government began democratic reforms. Ken Saro-Wiwa's death demonstrated to many people that almost without realizing it, they could be indirectly involved in restricting the freedom of people in other countries to act

Demonstrators outside a gas station in London. Ken Saro-Wiwa's death made many people aware of how big business may indirectly support oppressive regimes.

according to their beliefs.

Ken Saro-Wiwa's beliefs were not welcomed, his efforts to act on his beliefs denied. In curbing this right another human right was violated—his right to speak out, his right to freedom of speech (Article 19 of the Universal Declaration of Human Rights). Many of our human rights are interlinked in this way; when one is taken

Place: United States of America
Time: 1776
Issue: An agenda for the right to freedom of religious belief

In 1776, the 13 British colonies on the east coast of North America declared their independence from Britain. The colonists were not allowed to elect representatives to the British Parliament in London, and they believed that Britain had no right to rule over them from thousands of miles across the Atlantic Ocean.

After seven years of war, the colonies succeeded in gaining their freedom from Britain, and in 1787 they wrote a document called a constitution. This constitution set out how, from now on, the 13 States of America intended to govern themselves through their own new assembly called the Congress.

"no right to rule"

The final section of the American Constitution, called the Ten Amendments, or Bill of Rights, also laid down certain basic rights for all American citizens. The First Amendment made sure that everyone would have freedom of religious belief.

Although the American colonies did not formally declare their independence until 1776, fighting between British troops and colonists began in 1775. This illustration from the time shows the destruction of Charlestown.

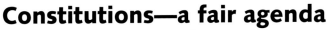

Constitutions—a fair agenda

The Constitution of the United States of America is one of the most important documents of modern times. It contains basic rules for the smooth government of the country; citizens must obey the laws of the land, but the government must make sure those laws are fair.

The rights of the citizens

The USA was the first country in the modern world to set out the rights of its citizens so clearly. Over the next 200 years it would influence governments in many other countries too, so that today most nations have some form of written constitution. The U.S. Constitution was also an important model for the United Nations, when it drew up the Universal Declaration of Human Rights in 1948.

(Above) Britain is one of the few countries in the world that does not have a constitution written down in a single document. Each year the British Parliament is opened by the monarch, but when it makes new laws it does not work from a formal document. Instead, it bases changes to British law on the traditions and practices that have gone before.

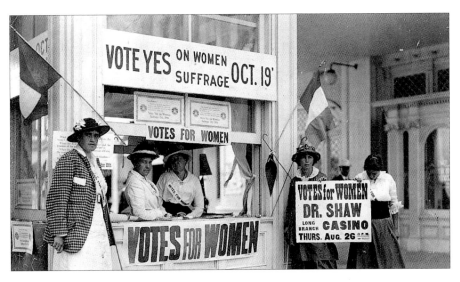

Constitutions and change

Although a constitution may grant all citizens certain inalienable rights—rights that cannot and should not be taken away by the government—in fact, as times, attitudes, and beliefs change, the constitution may have to change too. The U.S. Constitution now contains not 10, but more than 25 amendments, which have brought it up to date with new ideas and ways of looking at the world. The original Constitution, for instance, gave the right to vote in Congressional elections only to men. Yet by the early 20th century many people believed that women should be able to vote too. The 19th Amendment introduced equal voting rights in 1920.

(Above left) American women had a long struggle before they won the right to vote in federal elections. Known as suffragettes, women staged campaigns, such as this one in 1914, throughout the country. But it was not until 1920 that they gained the vote in the USA.

Governments and respecting beliefs

Of course, making changes to a constitution—and to the laws based on a constitution—is not an easy business. Although everyone now accepts that women should be able to vote, in 1920 there was much opposition to the move. Today other issues, such as euthanasia and abortion, arouse just as much debate and controversy, with people on both sides of the argument looking to the government or laws of the land to support their beliefs. Governments have to steer a difficult course around such issues, trying to understand and respect the freedoms of people with widely differing beliefs.

Governments have a difficult task in ensuring that the laws of the land are fair. Over time, laws are amended, dropped, or revised as the needs of societies and people change.

Euthanasia: a modern dilemma

Article 3 of the Universal Declaration of Human Rights says that everyone has the "right to life, liberty and security of person (the right to feel safe)." Most countries forbid killing, except in exceptional circumstances; perhaps as self-defense, or as a punishment for a violent crime such as murder. Yet is it wrong to kill someone who wants to die? In particular, what should an individual do if a sick friend or relative with a terminal illness asks for help to end his or her own life?

"debate and controversy"

The period after an operation in intensive care is very important (right). But what if the patient should fall into a coma or require a life-support machine for survival? Such machines can keep patients alive, even though they may be unconscious or unable to move, for months or years. In such circumstances, who should decide if or when to turn a life-support machine off?

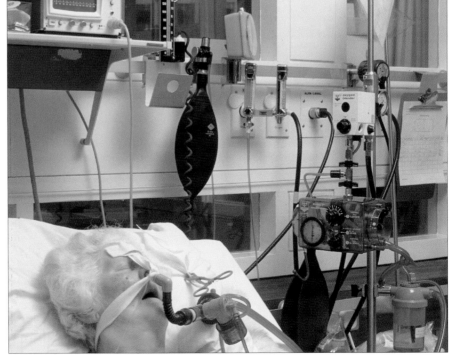

Place: Northern Territories, Australia
Time: 1996
Issue:
The strength of belief and a change in the law

In September 1996, Mr. Bob Dent, a 66-year-old Australian man, became the first person to die by a system of legally approved voluntary euthanasia. Mr. Dent was terminally ill, suffering from prostate cancer. He described his life as "a roller-coaster of pain."

Under the former state law, the Rights of the Terminally Ill Act 1995, Mr. Dent was able to receive the help of Dr. Philip Nitschke to end his life. Dr. Nitschke had previously developed a computer program that administers a lethal injection, through a line already put into the patient's arm, that is controlled by the patient. Mr. Dent died peacefully in his home in the presence of his wife and Dr. Nitschke.

Dr. Nitschke, seen with his computer program "Deliverance." The program is set up to ask the patient three "Yes/No" questions before the lethal injection is released.

Mercy killing

As medicine has advanced, it has become possible to keep some patients alive for much longer than ever before, even if that patient has no hope of recovery. Until recently, doctors who "helped" their patients to die were likely to be prosecuted for murder. The "right to life" has been understood to mean that human life should be preserved at all costs. Some people still support this viewpoint and feel that allowing "mercy killings" could open the way to abuse by unscrupulous governments, doctors, or relatives. They fear that legalizing euthanasia is the first step on a road toward getting rid of the old when they cannot look after themselves.

"prosecuted for murder"

Yet particularly in the western world, many other people now believe that euthanasia may not be wrong in some circumstances. They support the idea that, if they are seriously ill, individuals should have the "humane right" to end their lives as they wish. Euthanasia is legal in the Netherlands, Switzerland, Belgium, and in the state of Oregon.

The feeling among Australian citizens about becoming the first nation with a state that has legalized voluntary euthanasia was very mixed. Eventually, the Terminally Ill Act was overturned by the Australian Parliament in 1997. Bob Dent and three other terminally ill persons used the legislation to die before it was repealed.

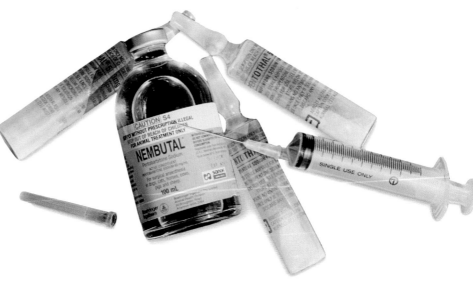

The dose delivered by Dr. Nitschke's program is a mixture of barbiturates and muscle relaxant to stop involuntary muscle movements once the patient is unconscious. The drugs are supplied through a line put into the patient's arm.

A careful compromise

The Netherlands has tried to deal with the controversial issue of euthanasia and the law for some time. In 1980, in response to the support for euthanasia, the Dutch Supreme Court ruled that euthanasia would be allowed in strictly controlled circumstances. While it is still technically illegal to end someone else's life, doctors are not prosecuted if they "assist" in a patient's death as long as they follow strict guidelines. The Dutch government feels that not altering the law to legalize all "mercy killings," however, makes sure that each case of euthanasia will always be treated with the respect and attention it deserves.

Is the Dutch ruling apparently contradictory, creating a confusing situation? Or is the government trying to make careful compromises that try to acknowledge and respect the beliefs of both supporters and opponents of euthanasia?

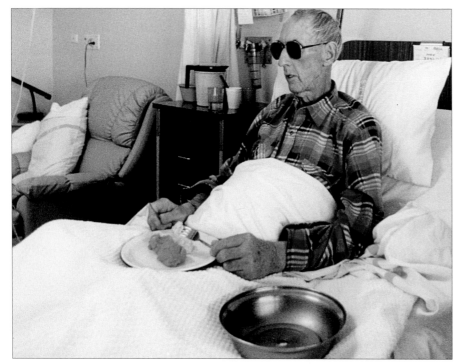

A patient waits for three doctors to agree to sign the forms to allow him to die under the 1996 state law in Australia.

A question of ethics

Abortion is another issue about which people have strong beliefs. Since 1967 in the UK and the 1970s in the USA and in some European countries, it has been legal for women to have an operation to end a pregnancy. This operation, called an abortion, takes the embryo, or unborn baby, out of the mother's womb in the early stages of development so that it cannot survive.

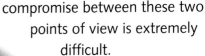

"a fundamental right"

Some women demanded abortion as a fundamental right; they saw it as an essential part of having control over their own bodies. However, other people think that abortion is wrong. They believe that a human being exists from the very moment a pregnancy begins. To stop a pregnancy once the embryo is fertilized is the same as killing someone who has actually been born. They would like to see abortion become illegal again. Finding a compromise between these two points of view is extremely difficult.

Before abortion became legal in many countries, women desperate to terminate a pregnancy sought illegal, "backstreet" abortions. These were often performed by people with no medical experience. It is argued that to avoid this happening again, abortion should remain or become legal and women should have proper medical counseling before having the operation.

The question of when a human embryo qualifies for protection according to human rights laws is the cause of many heated debates. Some believe it is at the point of conception and that abortion takes away a new life.

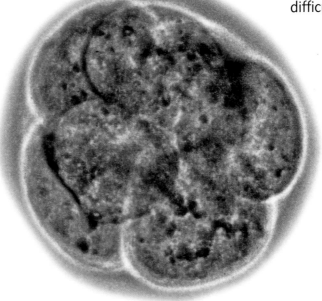

Time: 1993-4
Place: Pensacola, Florida
Issue: conflicting opinions and breaking the law

The Ladies' Services Clinic at Pensacola is one of the few clinics in that part of Florida that performs abortions. On many occasions, local activists who oppose abortion have demonstrated against the work performed at the clinic and the people who work there.

In 1993 Dr. David Gunn, a doctor who performed abortions at the clinic and for Pensacola Medical Services, was shot in the back three times by Michael Griffin. The clinic continued to offer abortions, with doctors wearing bulletproof jackets, but in 1994 another medic, John Baynard Britton, was shot dead through the head.

Before Michael Griffin came to trial, his supporters issued a statement: "We assert that if Michael Griffin did in fact kill David Gunn, his use of lethal force was justifiable provided it was carried out for the purpose of defending the lives of unborn children."

Michael Griffin, under arrest after having been charged with the murder of Dr. David Gunn after the shooting at the clinic in Pensacola.

The strength of feeling about abortion has often led to conflict in the United States. The Ladies' Services Clinic at Pensacola was destroyed by anti-abortion activists on December 24, 1984.

"defending the lives of unborn children"

Strength of feeling

The vast majority of Americans who oppose abortions have been horrified by the murders of the Pensacola doctors. Yet the Pensacola killings do show that certain people will go to almost any lengths (risking even imprisonment and their own execution) in an effort to have the law changed to reflect their own beliefs about what is right and wrong.

Creation theory and education

Like euthanasia and abortion, religion is an area that causes huge conflict of opinion. For this reason, parents are often anxious to educate their children in line with their own religious beliefs.

In the USA, some people do not accept the theory of evolution—the concept that species, including humans, evolved from simple life forms over millions of years. They believe traditional Christian teaching that God created the world in six days, resting on the seventh. They do not want their children taught the theory of evolution in biology lessons.

In the 1980s, to acknowledge these differing views the state of Arkansas tried to introduce the teaching of both these views side by side. This went against U.S. law, which, in an effort to respect all religions, did not allow government funding for educational programs that put forward just one set of religious beliefs, so the policy was rejected.

(Left) This Victorian cartoon made fun of Darwin's theory of evolution, which suggested that humans and apes had a common ancestor.

(Above) The theory of evolution caused controversy when it was first published, and it is still not accepted or taught by some schools in the United States today.

Strength of feeling is so strong among parents, however, that some state schools have decided not to teach evolution theory rather than risk upsetting the majority of the parents.

This situation opens up a large area of debate. Is this a case of individuals, rather than **"conflict of opinion"** governments, finding ways of dealing with conflict? Or are some children being denied the freedom to consider a different viewpoint? By not teaching evolution theory, are parents and teachers actually restricting their pupils' freedom of belief?

COMMUNITIES IN CONFLICT

Place:
Ayodhya, India
Time:
1992
Issue:
Strong beliefs and bitter confrontation

On December 6, 1992, a huge crowd of 100,000 Hindus attacked a 500-year-old, disused Muslim mosque in the northeastern Indian town of Ayodhya. They believed that the mosque stood on the birthplace of the Hindu god, Rama, and they wanted to build a Hindu temple on the site instead. The destruction of the mosque set off a wave of rioting between Hindus and Muslims across India leaving thousands of people dead.

India has experienced such communal violence on religious grounds before. In 1947, when India became independent from Britain, the country was partitioned into three, with two parts being made into a new country specially for Muslims, called Pakistan. At the time of Partition, half a million people were killed in fighting between Muslims, Sikhs, and Hindus. To try and stop such clashes ever

happening again, the Indian government said it would always try to treat the Muslim and Hindu religions fairly.

After 1947 the government kept the Ayodhya mosque locked, but in 1986 it was opened again so that Hindus could visit the site. India's ruling political party (the Congress Party) allowed this reopening to try and win votes from Ayodhya's large Hindu population. Local Hindus were already showing signs of switching their political support to Congress's main political opponents, the BJP, and this rival party had encouraged a popular demonstration against the closure of Rama's birthplace.

"tension between communities"

Hindu rioters attack the mosque at Ayodhya.

Although there is sometimes tension between India's Hindus and Muslims, the two communities have often lived peacefully together. The Taj Mahal, completed in 1648, was built by the Muslim Moghul emperor, Shah Jahan, who included many Hindus in his government.

The events of 1992 showed clearly how it was still possible for violence to break out between members of India's two main religious groups—especially when tensions between the different communities were aggravated by politicians in search of supporters.

Communities of belief

In many parts of the world different communities of belief live side by side—in the same countries, towns, and villages. Indeed, some of the richest cultures have come about because of the blending of different communities. Yet some of the most bitter conflicts also take place between people who live in the same place. The recent killings by antiabortionists in the USA show what may happen when individuals clash over passionately held beliefs. Such violence becomes far more widespread and devastating when whole communities are involved.

Muslim and Hindu aspects of life in a more harmonious union—an Indian Muslim prays while a cow, an animal that is sacred to Hindus, wanders by.

Divided by beliefs and race

Yugoslavia was formed after the First World War, as a federation (or group) of several small states in southeastern Europe. From 1945 to 1980, the country was ruled by General Tito, who had led Yugoslavia's resistance to the Nazis and become a powerful Communist dictator. After Tito's death, politicians tried to gain control of Yugoslavia. In the states of Serbia and Croatia some leaders appealed to people's sense of local identity to gain support: Serb leaders won favor by saying that Serb people in Yugoslavia were being treated unfairly; Croatian leaders won support by saying that Croatia should be independent.

By 1992, Yugoslavia had broken up as some states declared their independence and others joined up with Serbia. Serbia and Croatia went to war over where the border between the two states should be.

The distribution of peoples in the states of the former Yugoslavia at the outbreak of trouble in 1992.

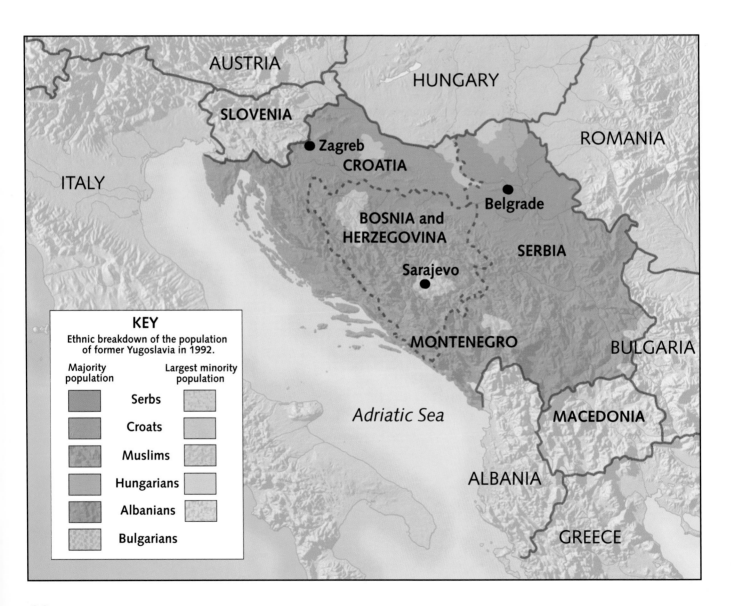

KEY
Ethnic breakdown of the population of former Yugoslavia in 1992.

Majority population | Largest minority population

Serbs

Croats

Muslims

Hungarians

Albanians

Bulgarians

Upsetting the balance

The central part of Yugoslavia was Bosnia and Herzegovina. Its ethnically mixed population was made up of 30% Serbs (who are mostly Orthodox Christians), 20% Croats (mostly Roman Catholics), and 40% Muslims from both Croat and Serbian ethnic backgrounds. Throughout Bosnia, some areas were mainly Serb, others Croat or Muslim. In many villages and towns all three groups lived together peacefully. Sadly, the fighting in other parts of former Yugoslavia upset this peaceful coexistence.

(Above) Mostar prior to the outbreak of war. The former Yugoslavia was very popular with tourists—offering a warm climate, beach vacations, and culture.

(Below) The same part of Mostar, but this time showing some of the visible effects of war—the bridge destroyed and buildings in ruins.

"ethnically mixed population"

In a referendum in 1992, most Bosnian Croats and Muslims decided it would best for Bosnia to become independent. Yet many Serbs in Bosnia were frightened about what would happen to them. They feared that an independent Bosnia would be influenced by Croatia, and wanted to join Serbia instead.

With the help of Serbia, a Bosnian Serb army was formed, which occupied most of Bosnia, and civil war broke out between Bosnian Serbs and the Bosnian Muslims and Croats. At one point, the fighting got even worse because the Croatian and Muslim armies also began fighting each other to control certain areas of the country.

Place:
Sarajevo, Bosnia
Time:
1991-1996
Issue:
Opposing beliefs
and the division
of a community

Zlata Filipovic was just 11 years old when her home in the center of Sarajevo (Bosnia's capital) came under attack from the Bosnian Serb army in 1991.

Many of Zlata's friends and family left Sarajevo just before the war reached them. Others, including one of Zlata's best friends, were killed in the bombing.

Zlata kept a remarkable diary of life in war-torn Sarajevo, which was published in Bosnia in 1993. It was translated and became a bestseller, explaining the horrible reality of the Bosnian war to people all around the world.

"Why is politics making us unhappy"

Zlata Filipovic's diary brought the attention of the world to the plight of ordinary young people living in war-torn Sarajevo. It highlighted the tragedy of local communities being torn apart.

Zlata herself is classed as a Croat but her family includes Catholic Croats, Bosnian Muslims, and Serbs. Zlata's diary expresses the frustration and despair of seeing the different groups in her community split apart: "Among our friends are Serbs, Croats, and Muslims…. Why is politics making us unhappy, separating us, when we ourselves know who is good and who isn't? We mix with the good…and among the good there are Serbs, Croats, and Muslims."

How can three communities that have lived peacefully together suddenly be at war? In Bosnia there seem to be two main reasons. First is the influence of politicians who stirred up tensions between the communities to win support for themselves. Second is the effect of fear—fear of persecution based on people's ethnic background and religious beliefs.

A stark illustration of opposing views as men are held captive by their oppressors —divided by their beliefs and race.

Concentration camp conditions meant that many prisoners starved to death.

A tragic result of conflicting beliefs

Civil war in Bosnia brought terrible destruction. Thousands of people were killed. More than two million Bosnians fled their homes. As Muslims fled from Serb or Croat-controlled areas, so Serbs fled from Croat regions and Croats fled from Serb-controlled areas. Worst of all was the "ethnic cleansing." Tens of thousands of members of the different communities were rounded up by the opposing armies and put in concentration camps: sometimes large groups of people were shot.

Faced with the collapse of the old Yugoslavia, and seeing the fighting between Serbia and Croatia, many Bosnians feared that their own community would come under threat. They were frightened that the particular community and tradition that their family came from might suffer discrimination—that they would be given the worst jobs, houses, or schools, for example. As each community's fear grew, it became more suspicious of the other two.

The tragedy of Bosnia is captured in this photograph of a grieving woman.

Peace for Bosnia?

The 1995 Dayton Peace Accords signed in the USA ended the Bosnian conflict, and was reinforced by the intervention of NATO troops. The multinational peacekeeping force still numbered around 12,000 in 2005 and weapons were still being collected. These soldiers work with the Bosnian military, local police, and international organizations to keep the peace and build a stable government. This cooperation gives Bosnia's different communities the chance to live together peacefully once again, free from discrimination because of their race or religion.

If Bosnia is to have a peaceful future, much rebuilding will be needed. Above all, the different communities will somehow have to rebuild their trust in one another.

"free from discrimination because of race or religion"

Place:
United States/
Northern Ireland
Time:
2003
Issue:
Moving beyond
fear and
prejudice

Claire Hanna, a student from Northern Ireland, discovered that the best way to overcome religious prejudice is to get to know the people you fear. Now on a scholarship at Georgetown University in Washington, D.C., she recalled growing up in Northern Ireland. "For us," she said, "the most important thing to learn when meeting someone new was which side they were on."

Then she participated in The Children's Friendship Project for Northern Ireland (CFPNI), a U.S. summer program that places two teenagers—one Catholic and one Protestant—together in American homes. CFPNI was established in 1987 to promote friendship and understanding. More than 2,000 teenagers have so far participated.

Claire's CFPNI partner was Victoria. Claire said that before they had met "Victoria was a Protestant to me before she was a person. "When they met, her opinion quickly changed.

Friendships between Catholics and Protestants are hard to make in areas of Northern Ireland, such as Belfast (above). But, as Claire Hanna discovered: "Away from that environment our beliefs were no longer important. As we began to see our similarities we became more accepting and understanding of our differences."

Graffiti in Northern Ireland, supporting Nationalists (above) and Unionists (below).

Understanding differences

In Northern Ireland a friendship between a prominent Catholic and a well-known Protestant is a brave move: terrorist organizations have often attacked people who have links with the "other side." Yet such links are essential to build up a real understanding between the two communities—an understanding that communities with different beliefs can live side by side.

Fear and suspicion have dogged the communities of Northern Ireland for more than 30 years. Since 1969 this province of the United Kingdom has experienced extreme violence between Catholic and Protestant paramilitaries and security forces. More than 3,000 people have been killed and some 30,000 injured in the disputes. Both groups are allowed to practice their religion freely, so why have they fought each other?

Political differences and religious divide

In Northern Ireland the majority Protestant community was traditionally richer and more powerful than the minority Catholic one. The political balance of the area largely reflects the religious divide. Catholics felt discriminated against and many decided that they would prefer Northern Ireland to become part of the Republic of Ireland, which is mainly Catholic. Most Protestants want to remain part of the United Kingdom.

Breaking down the barriers

The Irish Republican Army (IRA) was formed as a terrorist organization to try to force the British government to unite Northern Ireland with the Republic. Unionist paramilitary organizations (of Protestant sympathy) were formed, which attacked Catholic targets.

Because of the violence, the two communities have become more suspicious of one another than ever before. Few Catholic and Protestant adults socialize with one another, and their children hardly ever go to the same schools. In the capital, Belfast, only 8 % of people live in mixed neighborhoods. However, the IRA declared

Supporters of a united country of Ireland hold the Irish flag and make their beliefs known as they join a demonstration in Northern Ireland.

"Forge a way forward for peace"

ceasefires in 1995 and 1997, followed by the signing of the Good Friday Agreement on April 10, 1998 by eight political parties. This established a new Northern Ireland Assembly, providing the first home rule since 1974 with safeguards for minority rights.

Decommissioning of some IRA weapons occurred but delays in further disarmament led to the assembly being suspended from October 15, 2002.

After the IRA announced its ceasefire in September 1997, another group called the Real IRA, bombed Omagh, killing 29 people and wounding more than 200. In October 2002, the Real IRA admitted causing the outrage and disbanded, giving hope for a peaceful future.

LIVING TOGETHER

Time:
2004
Place:
New York City
Issue:
A right to
freedom of
belief and
a right
to work

Kevin Harrington, a 53-year-old Sikh driver of an subway train in New York City, was transferred to another job in June 2004 because he wore a turban instead of the regulation transit cap. In his new job of moving trains in the yards he was allowed to keep his turban because he was out of the public eye. But Harrington, who converted to the Sikh religion 25 years ago, went to local newspapers and the publicity embarrassed New York City Transit officials. They gave him back his original job and are now reviewing the dress code to accommodate the American constitutional right to religious expression.

"right to religious expression"

However, other similar cases in the city are still unresolved. Four Muslim women who operated buses were reassigned in 2002 to bus yards because they would not wear regulation caps over their khimars (head coverings), and two Sikh police officers were dismissed for wearing turbans.

Today, Sikh police officers in Australia and the UK wear a specially designed police turban.

Freedom from discrimination

Accepting that Sikhs may wear their turbans at all times is an important way of putting freedom of belief into practice. For Sikh men, not being allowed to wear a turban is a restriction of religious freedom—and discriminates against them because of their beliefs.

This victory for equality also made it clear that treating everyone in exactly the same way is not necessarily the same thing as treating everyone fairly. Avoiding discrimination sometimes means taking the differences between people into account.

Many governments have come to realize that they must recognize and respect many different traditions if people are to live happily together. Some countries now have laws to stop people from being treated unfairly because of their race or religion.

Modern multicultural societies are made up of people of many different races and beliefs.

In 1993 President Bill Clinton tried to introduce new rules allowing openly homosexual people to become military personnel. However, there was strong opposition to this move. The President backed down over his reform plans, and in a compromise introduced a "Don't ask, don't tell" policy: military authorities may no longer actually ask military personnel if they are lesbian or gay—but military personnel should not admit to their colleagues that they are homosexual.

(Left) In an effort to remove the restriction on gay personnel joining the U.S. armed forces, this man supports a "lift the ban" campaign.

Sexual differences

Even where people are protected by law from racial or religious discrimination, they may still find themselves discriminated against because they are "different" in some other way.

Discrimination because of "sexual orientation"—treating people differently because they are homosexuals (men and women who prefer to have sexual relationships with members of the same sex)—has also led to heated debates.

Some people believe that homosexuality is wrong. Others believe that same-sex relationships should be treated exactly like heterosexual ones. In most western countries, the law falls somewhere between these two points of view.

In 1993, President Bill Clinton's plans to reform U.S. military policy about homosexuality aroused strong feelings, both for and against the issues raised.

Place:
USA
Time:
Since 1992
Issue:
A difference of opinion or a case of prejudice?

Colonel Margarethe Cammermeyer joined the U.S. Army in 1965. She served in the Vietnam War and was awarded several medals. In 1991, during a routine interview, she was questioned about her sexuality. She admitted to having a lesbian relationship and was discharged, in spite of her 26 years' service. The Army considered her homosexuality to be "inappropriate conduct."

Margarethe Cammermeyer took her case to court and was reinstated in 1994. However, other personnel who admitted that they were homosexual of their own free will before the "Don't ask, don't tell" compromise was introduced have not been so fortunate and have lost their jobs in the armed forces for good.

"Don't ask, don't tell"

In a bid to uphold their belief that they are entitled to equal opportunities, gay military personnel take their individual cases to be heard in the U.S. courts.

41

The value of freedom

As with the issues of abortion and euthanasia, the arguments about homosexuality highlight the difficulties surrounding freedom of belief. What for one person seems like a fundamental human right may run directly against someone else's religious or ethical beliefs. But in order to be sure that we are behaving fairly toward each other, we have to be honest with ourselves about what we believe and whether our beliefs are based on knowledge or built up through fear, ignorance, or prejudice.

However difficult it is to achieve, freedom of belief will always be worth struggling for. Without it, new ideas and discoveries become impossible; individuals may have to live in totalitarian societies where whole groups of citizens suffer discrimination or the devastating effects of civil war and communal conflict.

Throughout the world and through the ages, people have been moved to fight for their beliefs. The importance of being able to express opinions and practice religious beliefs is seen as a crucial right by the United Nations and upheld in the Universal Declaration of Human Rights.

"**prisoners of conscience**"

Addressing the issue of human rights

There are many international organizations set up specifically to uphold some or all of the human rights set out in the Universal Declaration of Human Rights. Amnesty International is one such organization. While it promotes all the rights in the Declaration, a large part of its work is campaigning for the release of "prisoners of conscience"—people who are imprisoned for their beliefs. Often they, like Ken Saro-Wiwa or Palden Gyatso, have spoken out against their governments in order to attain what they see as the right to true freedom of belief.

As individuals, we may work against the violation of human rights—either by joining a campaign to speak out against discrimination or by simply making sure that we act fairly in our day-to-day lives. We all need to challenge our own thoughts from time to time. As the world changes, governments need to amend their laws—and we also need to question our own thoughts, attitudes, and beliefs.

(Above) The symbol for Amnesty International. Peter Benenson, the founder of Amnesty International, quoted an old Chinese proverb: "Better to light one candle than curse the darkness."

The European Court of Human Rights, in Strasbourg, is playing an increasingly important role in upholding human rights issues throughout Europe.

Glossary

abortion: an operation that takes place in the early stages of pregnancy. The embryo, or unborn baby, is taken out of the mother's womb, preventing the pregnancy from continuing.

barbiturate: a drug that calms you or slows your body down.

BJP: The Bharatiya Janata Party, or Indian People's Party.

Communist: Communists base their political views on the writings of Karl Marx. They believe that the State, not private individuals, should control industry and agriculture, in order to create a more equal society where wealth is divided as fairly as possible.

concentration camp: a prison camp where large groups of people—often civilians—are gathered in wartime. The most notorious camps were those of Nazi Germany, where millions of people perished.

conscience: a person's conscience is their sense of what is right or wrong. When we say that everyone should have freedom of conscience, we mean that they should have the right to make up their own minds about what they believe is right or wrong.

constitution: the rules, or fundamental principles, according to which a country is governed.

corporate: a group of people who are united by a common interest. The term is often related to business, where a group of people have the power to make decisions on behalf of the company.

democratic: in a democratic country, all the citizens have a say in how the government is run, usually by voting for people who want to represent their community in a parliament.

dictator: a ruler who has absolute power and governs without an elected parliament.

discrimination: treating people differently from others. The Universal Declaration of Human Rights says that some kinds of discrimination are unfair; for example, it is wrong to discriminate against people because of the color of their skin or because of their sex.

ethics: the unwritten laws of what people believe to be right or wrong. If you think something is not ethical, you think it is wrong.

ethnic: concerning a person's race. An ethnic group is a group of people belonging to the same race and culture.

euthanasia: the act of bringing about a gentle and painless death. Voluntary euthanasia is when an old or sick person decides they would like to be allowed to die, rather than wait until they die naturally of old age or the disease from which they are suffering.

evolution: the theory that species of plants and animals were not created in their present state, but have evolved, or developed slowly, over millions of years.

federation: a group of states joined together to form a larger country. The United States of America is a federation.

glasnost: the Russian word for "openness" or "freedom." In the late 1980s, the Soviet leader, Mikhail Gorbachev, introduced a new policy of *glasnost*, allowing Soviet citizens to discuss their government freely and openly for the first time ever.

homosexual: a man or a woman who prefer to have sexual relationships with someone of their own sex.

humane: kind or compassionate.

manifest: to show or display. People manifest their beliefs in many ways—by going to religious festivals, through the clothes they wear, or the food they eat.

Nationalist: in Northern Ireland, a Nationalist is a person who believes that Northern Ireland should become part of the Republic of Ireland.

observance: the following of a law, tradition, or religious custom.

paramilitary: a person who belongs to an unofficial, sometimes secret, army. In Northern Ireland there are both Nationalist and Unionist paramilitary groups.

persecution: repeatedly attacking or treating someone badly.

prejudice: literally means to prejudge something. If you are prejudiced against something, it means that you have an unreasonable dislike of it without even having found out about it, or thought it through properly.

referendum: referring an issue to the people of the country in order for it to be settled by their vote.

sexual orientation: whether a person prefers sexual relationships with someone of the same or the opposite sex, or both.

suffragette: the name given to one of the women who campaigned in order to win the right to vote in national political elections.

terminal: when used in relation to an illness, it means that the particular illness has no cure and will cause the patient's, often premature, death.

terrorist: a person who will resort to violence and intimidation in order to get his or her way or to make a political point.

totalitarian: a totalitarian government is one that controls all aspects of citizens' lives and does not allow any kind of political discussion or opposition.

Unionist: in Northern Ireland, a Unionist is a person who believes that Northern Ireland should remain part of the UK.

United Nations: the international organization, founded in 1945, that tries to bring together all the world's countries to build up friendly relations between them.

Universal Declaration of Human Rights: a list of human rights put together by the United Nations in 1948. The UN believes that every citizen in the world should be able to enjoy these basic rights.

Useful addresses

American Civil Liberties Union
125 Broad Street, New York, NY
10004
www.aclu.org

Americans United for Separation of Church and State
1816 Jefferson Place, NW,
Washington, DC 20036
www.au.org

Amnesty International USA
322 8th Ave.
New York, NY 10001
www.amnesty.org

Applied Research Center
3781 Broadway
Oakland, CA 94611
www.arc.org

Canadian Civil Liberties
Association
Suite 200, 394 Bloor Street West
Toronto, ON M5S 1X4
www.ccla.org

Center for Human Rights
Education
P.O. Box 311020
Atlanta, GA 31311
www.accessatlanta.com/community/groups/chre/

The Council of Canadians
502-151 Slater St.
Ottawa, Ontario, K1P 5H3
Canada
www.canadians.org

Free The Children
1750 Steeles Avenue West, Suite
218
Concord, Ontario, L4K 2L7
Canada
www.freethechildren.org

Institute for First Amendment
Studies P.O. Box 589
Great Barrington, MA 01230
www.ifas.org

National Conference for
Community and Justice
71 5th Avenue, Suite 1100, New
York, NY 10003
www.nccj.org

INDEX

abortion 22, 25-6, 27, 29, 42
Abucha, General Sani 17
Africa 14
America, North 20; see also USA
   South 17
Amnesty International 43
animals, attitudes to 8
armed forces 40, 41; see also Bosnia
Article 18 (UDHR) 12
Asia 17
astronomy 9
Atlantic Ocean 20
Australia 23, 24
Ayodhya, India 28

Belfast, Northern Ireland 35, 37
Belguim 23
belief, restricting freedom of 6, 7, 8, 10,
   11, 12, 13, 14, 15, 17, 19, 27
Bill of Rights, US, 20
BJP, Indian political party 28
Bosnia 30-4
Bosnia and Herzegovina 31
Britain 20, 28, 37, 38; see also UK
Bruno, Giordano 9
Buddhism 6, 7
business 18, 19

Cammermeyer, Margarethe 41
Children's Friendship Project for
   Northern Ireland (CFPNI) 35
China 6, 7
Christianity 7, 27, 31
Church, Roman Catholic 9, 31, 32, 35,
   36, 37
Clinton, President Bill 40
Communists/Communism 6, 14, 15, 30
concentration camps 33
Congress, Indian political party 28
Congress, U.S. 20, 21
conscience, freedom of 12, 34
Constitution, U.S. 20, 21
Copernicus 9
corruption 19
Croatia/Croatians 30, 31, 32, 33, 34

death sentence 9, 15, 17, 22, 26
democracy 19
democratic governments 18
Dent, Bob 23, 24
developing countries 18
dictators 30; see also totalitarianism
discrimination 34, 36, 39, 40, 42

education 13, 14, 27
ethics 8, 12, 25, 42
ethnic cleansing 33

ethnic minorities 11
Europe 10, 19, 25, 30
   Eastern 16
euthanasia 22-4, 27, 42
evolution, theory of 27
executions 33; see also death sentence

Filipovic, Zlata 32
First World War 30
   II 10, 30
Florida 26
freedom of thought 9, 12

gays see homosexuals
Germany 10, 14
glasnost 16
God 13, 27
Gorbachev, Mikhail 16
Griffin, Michael 26
Gunn, Dr. David 26
Gyatso, Palden 6, 7, 8, 43

heterosexuals 40
Himalayas 6
Hinduism 7, 28
Hitler, Adolf 14
homosexuals 40-2
human rights 18, 42, 43; see also UDHR

India 6, 28
   Partition of 28
industry 18
IRA 35, 37
Ireland, Northern 35-7
   Republic of 35, 37
Islam 7; see also Muslims
Italy 9

Jews 11, 13

labor camps 6, 13
lesbians see homosexuals
living standards 15, 16
London, England 20

"mercy killing" 23, 24
military dictators 19
murder 22, 23, 26
Muslims 28, 31, 32, 33

Nazis, the 10, 14, 30
Netherlands, the 23, 24
Nigeria 17, 19
Nitschke, Dr. Philip 23
Northern Ireland see Ireland, Northern

Ogoni people 17
oil 17, 19
Orthodox Christians 31

Pakistan 28
paramilitary forces 36
Parliament, British 20
Pensacola 26
Poland 9
politicians 16, 18, 29, 30, 33
poverty 14
prisoners of conscience 43
prisons 6, 7, 17, 35, 43
Protestants 35, 36, 37

Rama, Hindu god 28
religion 6, 7, 8, 13, 27, 28, 31, 35-7, 38
religious beliefs 7, 13, 18, 20, 27, 33, 42
religious freedom 7, 12, 13, 14, 20, 34,
   36, 39
Rights of the Terminally Ill Act 1995 23,
   24
Russia 14; see also Soviet Union
   1917 Revolution 14

Sarajevo 32
Saro-Wiwa, Ken 17, 18, 19, 43
science 9
Serbs/Serbia 30, 32, 33, 34
sexual orientation 40
Sikhs 38, 39
speech, freedom of 19
Stalin, Joseph 15

thought, freedom of 12, 15, 16, 34
Tibet 6
Tito, General 30
torture 6, 13
totalitarianism 13, 14, 15, 42
trade 18

United Kingdom (UK) 25, 37; see also
   Britain
United Nations (UN) 11, 18, 21
Universal Declaration of Human Rights
   (UDHR) 11, 12, 18, 19, 21, 22, 43
USA 21, 25, 26, 27, 29, 40
U.S. Army 41

vote, right to 21, 22

war, civil 31, 42
   Vietnam 41

Yugoslavia 30, 31, 34